THE
LITTLE PEPPER
BOOK

Michelle Berriedale-Johnson

PIATKUS

Other titles in the series

The Little Green Avocado Book
The Little Garlic Book
The Little Lemon Book
The Little Apple Book
The Little Strawberry Book

© 1982 Judy Piatkus (Publishers) Limited
Reprinted 1983

First published in 1982 by Judy Piatkus
(Publishers) Limited of Loughton, Essex

British Library Cataloguing in Publication Data

Berriedale-Johnson, Michelle
The little pepper book.
1. Peppers
I. Title
641.3'5643   TX558.P/
ISBN 0-86188-215-6

Drawings by Linda Broad
Designed by Ken Leeder
Cover photograph by John Lee

Typeset by Avocet
Printed and bound in Great Britain
at The Pitman Press, Bath

CONTENTS

THE CAPSICUM PLANT

It may be known as a pepper, but that shiny, round, green or red vegetable that you buy in your local greengrocer's is not really a pepper at all. Or, to be more accurate, it is not a relative of the *piper nigrum*, or black pepper corn, which is ground in a pepper grinder and is used to season almost everything we eat.

Sweet bell peppers and hot chile peppers are both fruits of the capsicum plant, which is indigenous to South America. Capsicums are members of the Solanaceae family, to which the potato, eggplant, tomato and tobacco plants also belong. They were first called peppers by the early Spanish and Portuguese explorers who discovered that the natives of South and Central America used a fiery spice to flavour their food. This spice, obtained from crushing dried chiles, was similar in taste to the ground black pepper used in Europe, and so the explorers christened it 'pepper'.

The capsicum has been said to get its name from the Greek verb *kapto*, which means to bite or to swallow greedily, and this could refer to the biting quality of the hot chile pepper. However, there is another school of thought that maintains that the name derives from the Latin word *capsa*, meaning a case or container. This derivation not only seems more likely but has the backing of the *Oxford English*

Dictionary.

There is little agreement as to how the 'chile' of chile pepper should be spelt. The spelling 'chile' or 'chili' derives from the Spanish and 'chilli' or 'chilly' from the Aztec. However, 'chili' or 'chilli' normally refers to a specific type of dried ground pepper, whereas 'chile' refers to the fresh hot pepper.

The varieties of pepper differ in size and fleshiness, but are all, as the name capsicum suggests, hollow and shaped like a fat tube closed at one end by the stalk. The other end can be rounded or it can taper into a point. In size they vary from tiny hot chiles, no bigger than a fingernail, to bells as large as a man's hand. The skins are taut, quite tough and shiny, and inside is a fleshy membrane varying in thickness from less than $1/16$ inch in the tiny chiles to over ¼ inch in a large bell pepper. White fleshy ribs run up the inside walls of the peppers and they are covered with small, flat white seeds. The ribs and seeds are the

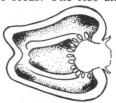

'hottest' parts of any pepper. The stalk is attached to a core which obtrudes into the middle of the fruit. This is made out of the same white flesh as the ribs and is covered with more white seeds.

The most active chemical constituent in the capsicum is capsaicin — a volatile carbolic compound which is closely related to vanillin, a component of vanilla. It is upon the quantity of capsaicin in each plant that the fieriness of the fruit depends. Bell peppers are relatively low in capsaicin (less than .001%), and the pungent chile peppers are high (approximately 1.3%).

There are 50 species of capsicums, which include annuals, short-lived perennials and both deciduous and evergreen shrubs. Capsicums are sensitive to frost and like good drainage; too much rain will cause rotting and poor fruiting. However, provided the soil is light and loamy, the rainfall over 25 inches a year and the drainage good, capsicums will grow almost anywhere.

All the species flower between June and August, producing whitish flowers about ¾ inch across with yellow stamens. The flowers last 2-3 days. Pollination is usually by bees and ants, and between 40-50% of pollinated flowers bear fruit.

In their natural habitat, the fruit will mature in August and September. However, the commercial value of bell peppers has increased dramatically since the Second World War and they are now grown in controlled conditions and available all year round.

Capsicums are prone to attack by glasshouse red spider mites which suck the sap of the plants in hot dry weather and cause mottling on the upper leaves; these eventually go bronze and drop off. The capsid bug can also cripple a growing plant and distort its leaves. However, regular spraying normally controls the pests and a lot of work is currently being done to develop disease and virus resistant varieties.

CULTIVATED VARIETIES

The most regularly cultivated peppers are those which fall into the categories of *Capsicum annuum* and *Capsicum frutescens*.

The species *Capsicum annuum* includes most of the edible capsicums.

The *Capsicum annuum grossum* is a shrubby perennial which seldom grows more than 18 inches high. Its fruit are the large glossy green bell peppers, which appear so regularly in our salad bowls. These green fruits eventually ripen to red or yellow. In Hungary, sweet red peppers are dried and powdered to make rose paprika.

The *Capsicum annuum acuminatum* is a slightly larger plant, also a perennial, and it produces the thin conical twisted fruits that are dried and used for making various hot peppers.

The *Capsicum annuum longum,* or long pepper, has a mild, drooping, red, yellow or ivory fruit, 8-12 inches in length.

The *Capsicum annuum cerasiforme,* or cherry pepper, has almost spherical red, yellow or purple fruit, ½-1 inch in diameter, with a pungent flavour.

The *Capsicum annuum concordes,* or cone pepper, has erect and conical fruit, approximately 1 inch long, and very pungent. Tabasco is derived from dried cone peppers.

The *Capsicum annuum fingerh,* or chile pepper, is a slim, pointed pepper over 3½ inches long, grown mainly in India and producing hot chili powder.

The *Capsicum frutescens* grows mainly in the tropics, where it can reach 6 feet in height. It produces blunt conical fruits which are extremely hot and acrid, often used for making very hot cayenne pepper.

NUTRITIONAL VALUE

The nutritional value of capsicums lies in their vitamin content. Vitamins A, C and E are present in sweet and hot peppers, the sweet peppers having particularly large amounts. Indeed, 1 ounce of raw sweet pepper contain approximately 40 mg of Vitamin C, which is two-thirds of the recommended daily intake of that vitamin. However, peppers lose their vitamin content when they are cooked or canned, or if they are allowed to get too ripe.

HISTORY OF THE CHILE PEPPER

The capsicum plant is indigenous to South America, where it grows wild. First cultivation of the plant is thought to have taken place around 7000 BC, and traces have been found at prehistoric burial sites in Ancon and Huaca Pieta in Peru. By the 15th century, when the Spanish and Portuguese arrived in South America, capsicums were in wide cultivation.

The Spanish found that the dried crushed fruits of the hot varieties made an excellent fiery substitute for the *piper nigrum* that they used so extensively in Europe. They called their discovery *pimienta* (Spanish for pepper), or *pimienta chilli* (as it was called in Mexico) to distinguish it from pepper corns, and they started to ship the fruit back to Spain.

The Portuguese went even further and sent capsicum plants to their settlements in the East Indies. On arrival, the new plant was rechristened Pernombuco pepper, and, since it was easier to grow and even hotter than the *piper nigrum*, it was soon well established. The chile pepper is now used as liberally in eastern cooking as it is in South American, and it is often thought, mistakenly, to have originated in the east rather than in the west, as did so many other fruits and spices.

The fruit spread rapidly throughout southern Europe where it found the climate much to its liking. Soon the powder ground from the dried fruits was being sold in all the major cities of Europe. It kept well and was easy to transport. In 1618, for example, one could buy it in Billingsgate in London, where it was known as 'Ginnie' or 'Guinea' pepper.

However, the powdered spice was very easy to adulterate with anything from oxide of red lead to coloured sawdust. And, as with so many exotic spices, the cayenne and chili peppers bought by the housewife in the 17th and 18th centuries were probably pale shadows of what we buy today.

Powdered chili pepper, or Guinea pepper as it was still called, appeared frequently in 18th-century recipes. However, it found its real enthusiasts among the Victorians who used it in the new Indian dishes which were so popular at the height of the British Empire in India. Varieties of the hot pepper were used even more often to give a kick or bite to the many bottled sauces and relishes which graced the Victorian dinner table. Harveys, Lazenbys and Crosse & Blackwell's were among the manufacturers.

In our own century, powdered chili pepper is used mainly in the preparation of national and ethnic dishes from as far afield as South America, California, India, China and Indonesia.

HISTORY OF THE BELL PEPPER

The fresh bell pepper came into its own in the 20th century. Although chili pepper powder was available as early as 1618, and despite the fact that the *Capsicum annuum* is a fairly tolerant plant and would no doubt have survived a northern climate as easily in the 17th century as in the 20th, there is no mention of it in the early English gardening manuals. Nor does it appear in any of the huge lists of fruit and vegetables for sale in Covent Garden market in the late 1600s. However, a variety did appear in Hungary in the 1580s, from which the sweet Hungarian paprika is derived.

Like the potato and the tomato, which also took a surprisingly long time to catch on, the bell pepper may have suffered from the fact that it belonged to the Solanaceae or Mandrake family. The mandrake was a root to which, in Britain in the Middle Ages, great healing powers were attached, and also much superstition. It was said to resemble the human shape and to shriek when it was pulled up. Moreover, many people believed that whoever dug it up would surely die. One can see how the other members of the mandrake family might have had a problem in getting themselves accepted!

The bell pepper was in regular use in the southern states of America by the mid 19th century and recipes for preserves, like the green pepper jelly we give, were quite common. It was also in common use in southern Europe where it grew easily, and, of course, in the far east and in South America where it originated.

However, the real explosion of bell pepper usage has come in the second half of this century with the arrival of fast refrigerated transport and the recent emphasis on health foods and salads. The bell pepper is at its best fresh and crisp in a salad. The enthusiasm with which its arrival in our salad bowls has been greeted has encouraged producers either to grow it in glasshouses in countries less than ideal for its cultivation, or to freight it in huge quantities from parts of the world where it grows happily. The result is that the peppers we buy now come from all over the world.

IMPORTS

In recent years Britain and the United States imported bell and chile peppers from over 60 different countries, including Spain and Portugal, the Netherlands, Italy, France, Romania, Hungary, Bulgaria, Egypt, Morocco, Canary Islands, Cyprus, Israel, Malawi, Sierra Leone, Kenya, Ethiopia, India, China, Malaysia, Papua New Guinea, Jamaica, Cuba and Venezuela. Interestingly, the smallest imports were from South America — the original home of the plant. There has been some attempt over the last few years to reduce the number of suppliers, but we still import peppers from the five continents.

Due partly to an excellent advertising campaign, the average Briton's consumption of fresh peppers increased dramatically between 1978 and 1980, although it has tailed off slightly since then. To illustrate the point: In 1977, we imported 66,132,000 kilos of sweet peppers, and this already impressive amount increased to an amazing 11,185,995,000 kilos in 1980! The major exporters are the Netherlands, Israel and the Canary Islands.

The consumption of fresh chile peppers has gone up during the same period but the increase has not been anywhere near as dramatic. In 1977, we imported 613,345,000 kilos of chiles and in 1980, 969,096,000 kilos — an increase of 355,751,000 kilos as opposed to an increase of 11,119,863,000 kilos of sweet peppers. Chile peppers are imported mainly from Spain, China and Papua New Guinea.

DECORATING WITH PEPPERS

Bell peppers can be used in fruit and flower decorations or as bright additions to a fruit bowl. Indeed, bowls of red, green and yellow peppers made of porcelain have become popular for sideboards and coffee tables.

Fresh chile peppers can also be used decoratively, and when they are dried the wrinkled fruits contort themselves into fantastic shapes and patterns.

There is also a small ornamental pepper plant which can be grown in a pot indoors; it has brilliant red fruits.

PEPPERS IN HEALTH AND MEDICINE

Sweet peppers are high in vitamins, particularly vitamin C. A report published recently by the American National Academy of Sciences shows that carotene, which is present in sweet peppers and is converted into vitamin A in the body, and vitamin C may offer some protection against cancers. Peppers could be very good for you indeed.

Sweet peppers contain large quantities of stearic and palmitic acids which produce essential oils important in the manufacture of soaps and candles. These essential oils are used as a lubricant in compressed tablets and pills; stearic acid is particularly useful in the manufacture of vanishing creams.

The oil content of the capsicum, if dissolved in ether and applied with cotton wool, is considered by many to be very useful in relieving rheumatic pains.

The main virtue of the chile pepper lies in the fact that it is a powerful stimulant, yet has no narcotic effects. For example, in an alcoholic it will stimulate the circulation and reduce dilated blood vessels without creating any further side effects.

It is interesting that the chile is most popular in tropical climates. The stimulation of the hot chile causes the heart to beat faster thus causing the body to sweat. Since the sweat glands are the body's natural air conditioner, the tropics are obviously the place to activate them!

Chile peppers, used with discretion, will also help a sluggish digestion. They certainly help the Mexicans and South Americans digest their heavy spicy foods. Most doctors in the 20th century agree that eating chiles, particularly the acrid *Capsicum annuum frutescens,* will encourage salivations, gastric secretions and gut movement and thus make food easier to digest. There is a West Indian recipe called Mandram which is also meant to help a weak digestion: chile pods are mixed with thinly sliced, unpeeled cucumber, shallots, chives or onions, lemon or lime juice and Madeira. Similar recipes appear in homeopathic and herbal medicine books.

It is even claimed by some that if one eats a lot of chile peppers they will rid the body of enough fats to lower the blood cholesterol level and reduce the chances of heart attack. Indeed, it is true that a study of chile-eating Spanish Americans has shown them to suffer from a remarkably low level of heart disease! However, if taken in excess, hot peppers can cause gastritis, renal irritation, inflammation and strangury.

The West Indians also use chiles in a gargle for a relaxed throat, mixing powdered cayenne pepper with boiling water. Again, this is a recognised homeopathic cure.

For hundreds of years, doctors, herbalists and quacks have been recommending chile pepper as a cure for digestive disorders, catarrh, weak sight, pimples and skin diseases, the ague, rheumatism, chilblains and alcoholism.

Culpeper, the great English herbalist who lived in the 16th century, recommended a powder made from a dry cake of Guinea pepper, flour and yeast. This powder 'when put into the diet, drives away wind and helps flatulency and taken in a cold stomach with meat, it gives great relief. It helps digestion, gives an appetite and provoketh the urine.'

No one suggests quite so many alternative uses for the plant as Culpeper. Other suggested uses for his 'pepper cake' include the following:

'The powder, taken fasting for three or four days, with a little fennel seed will ease all pains of the mother (at childbirth).'

'The powder, if applied with nitre, takes away freckles, spots, marks and discolourings on the skin.'

'A plaster, if made with the powder and tobacco, will heal venomous stings and bites.'

'A decoction of the husks (of the peppers) is a good gargle for the toothache and preserves the teeth from rottenness; and the ashes rubbed on the teeth will cleanse them.'

'The powder, if made up with turpentine and laid on hard knots and kernels in any part of the body, it will dissolve them.'

Maybe the best recommendation for the medicinal properties of peppers comes from a passage in Robinson's *New Family Herbal*, in which this letter from a Mr S. Thompson is quoted: 'In the fall of 1807 I was in Newburyport and saw a bottle of pepper sauce. Being the first I had ever seen I bought it, got some of the kind of pepper that was dried, which I put into the bottle. This made it very hot. On my way home I was taken unwell and was quite cold. I took a swallow from the bottle which caused violent pain for a few minutes, when it produced a perspiration and I soon grew well again.'

Later in the 19th century, Dr Kitchener, gastronome and author of the *Cook's Oracle*, was another enthusiastic supporter of the fiery pepper. The good doctor believed firmly in the invigorating qualities of the chile pepper and thought it a great aid to the digestion. He saw cayenne as a great thirst provoker which was, in the days when the consumption of enormous quantities of alcohol was seen as a necessary part of good living, a great virtue on its part.

THE BELL PEPPER IN THE KITCHEN

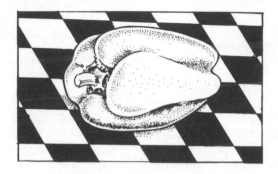

The bell pepper is one of the kindliest and most adaptable of vegetables. There is scarcely a country in the world which does not have its own version of stuffed peppers, although the more northerly ones, such as Scandinavia and Britain, have only recently discovered its delights.

Peppers have long been a constituent of many southern European dishes — from ratatouille to Hungarian gulyas — and now appear in the plainest of salads. Peppers are chopped and added to dips and cheeses; crushed into soups and sauces; sectioned and stuck on kebab sticks; pickled, jellied, bottled, canned and frozen. The sweet red pepper is even dried and powdered like its fiery cousins to make the rose paprika so beloved of Hungarian cooks.

BUYING PEPPERS

The ideal time of year to buy bell peppers is at their natural fruiting time in the later summer, but modern methods of cultivation keep them in the shops throughout the year. Fresh bell peppers should have firm, shiny, unwrinkled skins. Slightly elderly or wrinkled peppers can be used for cooking as their flavour lingers after their crispness has left them.

There is a multi-coloured range of peppers—green, red, yellow, ivory and purple. The most widely available are the red and green ones, the ripe and unripe versions of the same fruit. In fact, if you have a green pepper which you wish were red, you have only to wrap it in tissue paper and store it in a cool place for a few days and with luck it will turn crimson.

STORAGE

A bell pepper should last for at least a week if kept in the fridge. Once it is cut it tends to soften at the cut edges and should be used as soon as possible. Fresh peppers can be successfully frozen, but should first be cored, seeded and blanched. Once defrosted, they should be used immediately for cooking.

Canned or bottled peppers obviously have an indefinite shelf life, but, although they are delicious in salads or as hors d'oeuvres, their texture is soft and oily and quite unlike that of a fresh pepper.

PREPARING PEPPERS

For most salads and stews, bell peppers are used with their skins on. Careful skinning of the fruit does enhance its flavour without detracting from its texture. The skin of a pepper can give it a bitter flavour, particularly when it is cooked.

There are several ways to skin a pepper, but one of the best is to toast it carefully and evenly over a naked

flame or under an electric grill until the skin has blistered all over. Immediately wrap the pepper in a cloth which has been wrung out in hot water and put it aside for half an hour. Then rinse it under cold running water. Much of the skin will wash off, and the rest can easily be pulled off in strips.

The pepper, skinned or unskinned, should have its stalk, ribs and seeds removed. The easiest way to do this is to cut the pepper in half first.

The pepper is now ready for use.

ITALIAN CONSERVED PEPPERS

The Italians use the colourful yellow and red peppers with joyous delight, and in their high season will bottle and preserve them for use in the dark days of winter.

Buy large, fleshy and really ripe peppers and skin them by charring over a naked flame or under the grill and then washing off the skin under cold water. Make sure that all the skin is removed.

Cut the peppers in half, core, stalk and seed them. Pack them into preserving jars, sprinkling each layer lightly with salt and fresh basil leaves. Cover the peppers with good white vinegar and with a thin layer of olive oil. Screw down the lid tightly.

To serve, rinse the peppers in cold water and sprinkle each with a little good olive oil and some freshly ground black pepper.

Serve one pepper per person as a first course.

AJWAR

This recipe comes from Yugoslavia. It is very rich and makes a delicious first course when eaten with thickly cut fresh rye bread or brown toast.

oil for deep frying
2 large red peppers
6 thick slices of aubergine
3 large cloves of garlic
sea salt
freshly ground black pepper

Heat the oil in a deep frying pan until it is almost smoking.

Submerge the peppers in the oil for approximately 1 minute, or until they blister all over. Remove, cool slightly and skin. Remove the core, ribs and seeds and chop the peppers roughly.

Lightly fry the aubergine slices in a little oil.

Mince the peppers, aubergine and garlic in a food processor, mincer or liquidiser. Season to taste with sea salt and black pepper.

Serve with rye bread or brown toast.
Serves 6

GREEN PEPPER AND PRAWN SOUP

Although this appears to be a rather luxurious soup, it is neither expensive nor difficult to make — the perfect starter for a busy hostess!

6 spring onions
4 oz prawns in their shells
5 fl oz natural yoghurt
½ pint milk
juice of 1 lemon
1 stick celery, very finely chopped
1 medium-sized green pepper, cored and seeded and finely chopped
6 drops Tabasco
salt and white pepper

Clean and roughly chop 2 spring onions and put them in a pan with ½ pint water. Shell the prawns and add the shells to the onions and water. Bring to the boil and simmer for 15 minutes, strain and cool the liquid.

Mix the yoghurt, milk and lemon juice in a bowl. Add the celery, green pepper and remaining spring onions, cleaned and finely chopped, then add the Tabasco and the prawns. Pour in the cooled fish stock and season to taste with salt and white pepper.

Allow the soup to chill in the fridge for several hours — the flavours will amalgamate gradually as the soup chills.

Serves 4

PEPPERS AND CUCUMBER IN A YOGHURT DRESSING

The addition of mint and yoghurt gives this recipe a distinctly east European flavour; a lovely fresh starter for a summer dinner party.

1 medium-sized cucumber
1 teaspoon sea salt
4 medium-sized green peppers
3 finely chopped spring onions
1 tablespoon chopped fresh tarragon
1 tablespoon chopped fresh mint
½ pint yoghurt
freshly ground black pepper

Peel the cucumber and cut in thin slices. Spread the slices on a plate or in a colander and sprinkle them with salt. Place a plate with a weight on top over the cucumber for about 30 minutes to allow the excess liquid to drain off.

Core and seed the peppers and cut them in fine strips.

Put the peppers in a bowl with the cucumber and mix in the onions and herbs. Stir in the yoghurt. Season with black pepper and a little more salt if necessary.

Chill for 1 hour before serving on a bed of lettuce leaves.
Serves 6

RATATOUILLE

Ratatouille is one of the most popular of the Mediterranean vegetable dishes and there are many variations to be found. Use it as a starter, vegetable or salad.

4 tablespoons olive oil
2 medium-sized onions, peeled and thickly sliced
2 cloves garlic, crushed
2 red and 2 green peppers, cored, seeded and thickly sliced
2 aubergines, sliced in rounds
4 courgettes, sliced in rounds
salt and pepper
1 large can Italian tomatoes
1 packet plain potato crisps (optional)
2 oz grated parmesan (optional)

Heat the oil in a heavy based pan, add the onions, garlic and peppers and cook gently until they start to soften. Add the aubergines and courgettes and cook for a further 5 minutes.

Season with salt and pepper, then add the tomatoes, cover and simmer gently for approximately 30 minutes or until all the vegetables are cooked. Adjust seasoning to taste.

You may now use the ratatouille hot as a vegetable or allow it to cool and use it as a salad.

Serves 6

SOUTH AMERICAN
STUFFED GREEN PEPPERS

These stuffed peppers make an unusual and attractive starter or main course.

8 small green peppers
1 medium-sized onion
1 oz butter
1 tablespoon oil
3 tablespoons brown rice
4 oz spicy sausage
1 clove garlic, crushed
1 tablespoon chopped parsley
1 egg
salt and pepper

Cut the tops off the peppers and remove the seeds and ribs. Season lightly with salt.

Peel and chop the onion and put in a saucepan together with the butter and the oil. Add the rice and ½ pint water. Bring to the boil and cook for 20 minutes, by which time all the water should be absorbed.

Mix the sausage, garlic, parsley and egg into the rice mixture. Season to taste with salt and pepper and spoon the stuffing into the peppers.

Wrap each pepper in aluminium foil and cook in a hot oven (210°C, 425°F, Gas Mark 7) for 20 minutes.

Serve warm or cold but not chilled.
Serves 8 for a starter, 4 for a main course

FRESH PEPPER SALAD

If you can find peppers in all the different colours your salad will look almost too good to eat!

1 small green pepper
1 small red pepper
1 small yellow pepper
1 small purple pepper
2 large sticks of celery, finely chopped
2 oz chopped walnuts
4 sprigs watercress, roughly chopped
sea salt
freshly ground black pepper
4 tablespoons olive oil
juice of 1 lemon

Seed and core the peppers and slice in rings. Arrange in a pattern around the edge of a serving dish.

Mix together the celery, nuts and watercress and pile in the middle of the dish.

Sprinkle the salad with salt and pepper, olive oil and lemon juice. Serve at once.
Serves 4

CHEESE STUFFED GREEN PEPPERS

This vegetarian recipe makes a delicious first course.

4 oz flour
1 egg
5 fl oz lager or beer
oil for deep frying
6 small green peppers
½ oz butter
2 sticks celery, very finely chopped
6 oz well-flavoured cheese, grated
small bunch chives, finely chopped
1 teaspoon Tabasco
2 egg whites

Beat together the flour, egg and beer to make a batter. Set on one side for at least 30 minutes.

Heat the oil until almost smoking. Lower the peppers (whole) into the oil and keep them completely submerged until they blister all over. This will take approximately 1 minute. Lift them out and allow them to cool slightly. Remove the skins and then cut the pepper open down one side. Carefully remove the core, ribs and seeds.

Melt the butter and soften the celery.

Mix together the cheese and chives, add the softened celery and season with Tabasco. Whisk the egg whites and fold them into the cheese mixture. Spoon the mixture into the peppers and 'sew' the two edges together with a cocktail skewer.

Coat each pepper liberally in batter and deep fry for 2-3 minutes. Drain and serve immediately.
Serves 6

PIMIENTO A LA TAMBERA

An unusual cold stuffed pepper dish — ideal for a summer dinner party or to take on a picnic.

3 red and 3 green peppers
6 tablespoons good mayonnaise
rind and juice of 1 lemon
5 hard-boiled eggs, roughly chopped
2 teaspoons whole-grain mustard
8 oz Cheddar cheese, grated
handful chopped parsley
salt and pepper

Put the whole peppers into a bowl of boiling water and keep submerged for 5 minutes. Lift them out and quickly run them under cold water. Halve them lengthways and remove the stalks, seeds and ribs.

Meanwhile, mix the mayonnaise with the lemon rind and juice and stir in the eggs. Add the mustard, cheese and parsley and seasoning.

Pile the mixture into the pepper shells and serve on a bed of lettuce. Serve one red and one green half per person.
Serves 6

GREEN PEPPER AND MINCE PIE

This is a very useful recipe as the pie is just as tasty cold as it is hot, and when made up into individual pasties is ideal to take on a picnic.

1 tablespoon bacon fat
2 small onions, peeled and roughly sliced
2 small green peppers, cored, seeded and roughly sliced
12 oz minced beef
3 tablespoons tomato purée
1 tablespoon Worcestershire sauce
2 tablespoons red wine
salt and pepper
8 oz shortcrust pastry

Melt the bacon fat in a pan and briskly fry the onions and peppers for 3 minutes without burning. Add the mince, mix well and continue to fry for a further 5 minutes. Add the tomato purée, Worcestershire sauce and red wine and season to taste with salt and pepper.

Line a flan dish or small pie dish with two-thirds of the pastry, pile in the meat mixture and cover with the remaining portion of pastry.

Brush with the beaten egg and bake in a moderate oven (180°C, 350°F, Gas Mark 4) for 30 minutes or until the pastry is cooked and golden.

Alternatively, roll out the pastry and make into one large or several small pasties. Bake as for the pie.
Serves 4

CHICK PEAS WITH CHILES AND GREEN PEPPERS

A filling and tasty vegetarian dish which makes a cheap but nourishing supper. It uses both mild and hot peppers.

8 oz chick peas
2 fresh green chiles or 4 small dried red chiles
3 tablespoons olive or cooking oil
2 medium-sized onions, peeled and roughly chopped
2 cloves garlic, finely chopped
1 large green and 1 large red pepper, cored, seeded and
    roughly chopped
2 large tomatoes, roughly chopped
juice of 1 lemon
salt and pepper

Soak the chick peas in water overnight. Drain and put in a saucepan with approximately 2 pints cold water. Bring to the boil and simmer for 40 minutes or until the peas are tender but not mushy. Drain and set on one side.

If the chiles are fresh, core and seed them and chop roughly; if they are dried, slice them very finely.

Heat the oil in a heavy based pan, add the onions, garlic and peppers and fry them gently for 5 minutes without burning. Add the chick peas, tomatoes, lemon juice and seasoning to taste. Cover and simmer for 20 minutes.

Serve hot or cold.

Serves 4

HUNGARIAN GULYAS

The best known of all bell pepper recipes.

1 oz lard
5 oz onions, finely chopped
1 clove garlic, finely chopped
4 tablespoons sweet Hungarian paprika
2 lb shin of beef, cubed
1 teaspoon caraway seeds
1½ pints chicken or beef stock
½ teaspoon salt
freshly ground black pepper
4 medium-sized potatoes
1 lb tomatoes, peeled, seeded and chopped
4 small red peppers, cored, seeded and halved
½ teaspoon marjoram
5 fl oz sour cream

Heat the lard in a heavy saucepan and add the onions and garlic. Cook for about 10 minutes or until lightly browned. Remove from the heat. Stir in the paprika.

Add the beef, caraway seeds and stock to the onion mixture and season with salt and pepper. Bring to the boil, partially cover and simmer for 1 hour, or until the beef is almost tender.

Parboil the potatoes in their skins until they can be penetrated with a knife to about ¼ inch. Peel them and cut them into cubes.

Add the potatoes, tomatoes, peppers and marjoram to the saucepan, partially cover and cook for a further 25 to 30 minutes. Add the sour cream and adjust the seasoning.

Serves 6

PEPPER PIZZA

Pizza dough is a good base for a mixture of sweet and fiery peppers. If you do not want to go to the trouble of making pizza dough, a shortcrust pastry flan case will make a very acceptable substitute.

2 small green peppers, sliced
2 small red peppers, sliced
1 large onion, sliced
2 small green chiles, finely sliced
3 cloves garlic, crushed
4 tablespoons olive oil
6 oz mozzarella, ricotta or edam cheese, diced small
salt and pepper
4 oz prepared pizza dough, or baked flan case

Fry the peppers, onion, chiles and garlic in the oil for about 5 minutes, or until they are slightly softened. Mix in the cheese and season with salt and pepper.

Pile the mixture onto the pizza dough or into a flan case and cook in a hot oven (210°C, 425°F, Gas Mark 7) for 8 minutes or under a grill for 4.

Serve at once.
Serves 8

ESCOFFIER'S PEPPER CHUTNEY

This unusual French condiment goes very well with traditional meats such as roast lamb or pork. It is especially good served with cold meat.

1 lb onions, finely chopped
2½ lb green peppers, cored, seeded and chopped
2 tablespoons olive oil
2 lb very ripe tomatoes, peeled and chopped
1 clove garlic, crushed
1 teaspoon ground ginger
1 lb sugar
8 oz sultanas
1 teaspoon mixed spice
1 pint wine vinegar

In a covered saucepan, simmer the onions and peppers in the oil for 15 minutes. Add the remaining ingredients and cook very slowly for 3 hours.

Cool and pot.
Makes 3-4 lbs chutney

GREEN PEPPER JELLY

This brilliantly coloured jelly has long been a great favourite in the American south.

4 green peppers, seeded
1 red pepper, seeded
½ pint cider vinegar
1½ lb granulated sugar
½ teaspoon salt
juice of 2 lemons

Mince the peppers and drain them well.

Place the peppers and the remaining ingredients in a saucepan, bring to the boil and simmer for 10 minutes. Test for consistency as for a fruit jam; if not sufficiently set, continue to boil for a further 5-10 minutes, testing continually.

Add a few drops of green colouring if desired.

Pot in jars as for jam.

Makes approximately 2 lb jelly

HOT PEPPERS

The chile pepper has been cultivated in South America for nearly 10,000 years so it has had plenty of time to evolve. As a result, there are almost as many types of chile pepper as there are days in the year. These are just some of the chiles regularly grown in Mexico alone: Ancho, mulato, pasilla, serrano, jalapeño, guajillo, cascabel, pequin, chiltepin, carrecillo or tornachile, hanaera, cora, guajon, bola, gordo, arribeno, guero, costeno, arotonilco, huachinango, puya, cristalino, trompa, bolita, catalina, ornamental, chile de ague, liso, pinalteco, zacapeno, San Luis, loco, chircozle, pimiento, chile de arbol, poblana, chilaco, chiguacle, chiclateco, mihuateco, chile mirasol rojo.

Although chile peppers are by their very nature hot, some are hotter than others! A good rule of thumb is that the smaller the pepper, the darker the colour, the more pointed the top and the narrower the shoulders, the hotter it will be. A number of different types of chile pepper are imported and sold but, as they are seldom named, this is quite a useful tip to remember.

Despite this emphasis on their heat and fiery nature, the different varieties of chile pepper do have very specific flavours of their own. Should you find yourself with a selection of chiles in front of you, this is what some of them may be:

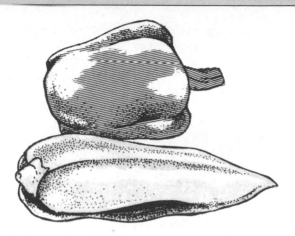

Ancho — one of the most widely used peppers, especially in Mexico and the United States. It is about 4 inches long and 3 inches wide, and a fresh ancho looks like a bell pepper. When ripe, it darkens to a very deep, almost black, red. It is rich, full and relatively mild in flavour.

Mulato — similar in shape and size to an ancho, but longer, more tapering and almost brown in colour. Mulato is wrinkled and more pungent than ancho.

Pasilla — this pepper is 6-7 inches long and only 1 inch wide. It is a very dark red, very richly flavoured and *very* hot. It is sometimes called chile negro because of its dark colour.

Serrano, jalapeño, pequin, cascabel and tepin peppers are all small, dark green, tapering and between 1½-2 inches long. They are all *very hot indeed,* although the heat resides in the ribs and seeds rather than the flesh. They are difficult to find fresh, but most gourmet shops store pickled and canned varieties.

Malagueta peppers come from Brazil and are sometimes called cayenne chiles. They are small and hot. The ripe pepper is bright red and rich in flavour, and is sold fresh.

The *habanero* peppers of Mexico also grow in tropical Brazil, and in Jamaica where they are called Scotch bonnets! Their flavour is much prized and they are often bottled for long keeping.

Chile peppers from the East Indies and from Africa fall into approximately the same categories, but care should be taken to avoid a small Japanese pepper called *Hortoka*. This is pure liquid fire — indeed, an eighth of a teaspoon of hortoka is the equivalent of one whole pequin pepper, one of the hottest of the Mexican breeds . . .

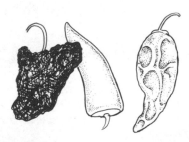

CHILI, CAYENNE, PAPRIKA AND TABASCO

M any people will have only met chile peppers in the form of ground cayenne, chili or paprika pepper, or as Tabasco. These powders are made by crushing the dried peppers, usually complete with ribs and seeds; the variation comes in the fruit that is crushed. The sweet Hungarian paprika, which is very mild in comparison with its fiery cousins, is made from several different varieties of the *Capsicum annuum grossum*.

What we buy in the shops as chili powder comes mainly from India and is usually derived from the *Capsicum annuum Fingerh*. Cayenne pepper can be made both from the *Capsicum annuum acuminatum* and the *Capsicum annuum frutescens*. The chief growing area is French Guiana, and the capital city of French Guiana is Cayenne!

Tabasco (which is a trade name rather than a botanical one) is the only one of these spices to come in liquid form. Powdered *Capsicum annuum concordes* is mixed with spirits of vinegar and salt to create a lethal liquid which is contained in little glass bottles.

All these peppers are excellent for seasoning dishes, but they are, with the exception of paprika, extremely hot and should be used with discretion.

BUYING GROUND PEPPERS

Ground and pre-prepared chile peppers (chili, cayenne and paprika) are easily available. However, like all spices, they can be adulterated and very quickly become stale. Always ensure that you buy a pure spice (many are blended with oregano, cumin, salt, garlic and masa flour). The peppers should be properly packed in airtight, opaque containers as contact with air and light causes the pepper to oxidise, thus evaporating the flavour of the chile and leaving only the hotness.

Pure chili powder, or cayenne, should be powerful and concentrated, so unless you have an asbestos mouth and a well-trained family, add it to food in very small quantities at first — you can always add more later. If you do add too much, a little sugar sprinkled over the dish will take away some of the hotness.

◆

HANDLING TIPS

When one talks about hot peppers one thinks always of a burning sensation in the mouth. However, if you are handling fresh chiles you must remember that the oils and juices in the flesh will burn your fingers as successfully as they will burn your tongue. They must be treated with great care.

*Wear rubber gloves, especially if preparing the hotter varieties. Some people say that 'buttering' your hands will protect them, but rubber gloves are a great deal more efficient.

*When you have finished preparing chiles, wash both the gloves and your hands very thoroughly with soap and warm water.

*NEVER TOUCH YOUR EYES, NOSE OR MOUTH until you have washed your hands and gloves. The skin in these areas is very sensitive and will react painfully to any contact with the peppers.

*If you do burn yourself with the chile, treat the burn as you would any other burn. Run it under cold water and dress it with a baking powder paste or a burn ointment.

Dried chiles do not present the same hazards in handling as they lack the volatile oil present in the fresh fruit. Nonetheless, they should be treated with respect!

Preparing Chiles
For Use

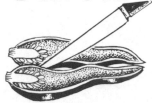

Fresh Chiles

One having donned one's rubber gloves, chiles may be cut in half lengthways and the seeds and ribs removed. Preferably, this operation should be done under running water. The flesh can then be sliced or chopped into whatever size is needed.

Alternatively, the flesh, ribs and seeds can be minced or pulverised to make a really hot chile sauce.

Chile peppers, like bell peppers, benefit from skinning. There are various methods but the method given below skins and seeds the pepper at the same time.

Rinse and drain the chiles and with the point of a knife, pierce each one (once) near the stem. Put the chiles on a baking tray and place under a hot grill, turning frequently until brown and blistered all over. Wrap in a cold damp towel and leave to steam for 10 minutes. Peel off the skin, downwards in long strips, then pull off the stem and, holding the point up, squeeze the pod from the point downwards and all the seeds will squirt out.

DRIED CHILES

Dried chiles can either be pulverised and used as a spice or reconstituted and used as a vegetable. To do this they need only be soaked for approximately 30 minutes in tepid water. This method can be used for whole chiles or chile pieces.

◆

THE RECIPES

Included are representative recipes from areas of the world where the chile pepper is regularly used. Because of the difficulty of getting all the different kinds of chile peppers, some of the recipes have been simplified. The quantity of chile has been reduced in several of the recipes in deference to unaccustomed palates!

The national cuisines which use chiles extensively vary greatly. In Central and South America, the chile is used to spice and lighten the heavy rice, bean and tortilla dishes which form the staple diet of the people. In China, chiles with salt and vinegar are incorporated in hot and spicy sauces; in South East Asia, Malaysia, Sri Lanka and Indonesia, the chile is more usually mixed into the dish with ginger and garlic and cooled with vinegar to give a sweet and sour flavour. In India, fresh chiles are served as an accompaniment to a curry, and in parts of Africa they make up a hot chile paste to use in cooking.

PRAWNS PIL PIL

Prawns pil pil is a favourite dish in southern Spain, where it is made with delicious fresh prawns. However, this recipe does have the virtue of giving some flavour to rather tasteless frozen prawns.

8 oz cooked prawns (if fresh, peeled; if frozen, thawed and well dried)
cayenne pepper
4 tablespoons olive oil
fresh crusty bread

Divide the prawns between four small ovenproof dishes and sprinkle lightly with cayenne pepper. Pour 1 tablespoon oil over each dish and place under a hot grill for 8-10 minutes.

Serve at once with plenty of fresh bread to mop up the oily juices.
Serves 4

MEXICAN FISH STEW

This chile and fish dish comes from Mexico, and the delicate flavour of the fish is actually enhanced by the hotness of the green chiles. Mexican fish stew is really a cross between a soup and a stew and should be eaten in bowls, like a bouillabaisse, with plenty of fresh bread.

2 medium-sized onions
1 lb tomatoes
6 small green chiles
2 bay leaves
3 cloves garlic, crushed
salt
1 teaspoon oregano
a sprig of fresh coriander, if possible
1½ lb white fish, haddock, whiting etc, filleted
3 greengages or 12 white grapes

Peel and chop the onions and tomatoes. Seed and chop the chiles. Put the vegetables in a saucepan together with the bay leaves, garlic, salt, oregano and coriander. Add 4 pints water and bring to the boil, then simmer until the onion is tender.

Skin the fish and add it to the pan. Cook gently for a further 10 minutes.

Slice the greengages, or halve and pip the grapes, and add to the pot. Continue to simmer for a further 10 minutes, or until the fish is cooked.

Serve at once.
Serves 6

SAMBAL GORENG KEMBANG
(Chile fried cauliflower)

This cauliflower dish comes from Malaysia and makes an excellent first course. Alternatively, you could spear the cauliflower pieces with a cocktail stick and serve them with drinks.

3 tablespoons peanut or walnut oil
4 fresh red chiles, finely chopped
1 large onion, finely chopped
2 cloves garlic, finely chopped
1 inch piece of fresh ginger root, peeled and finely chopped
1 teaspoon of shrimp paste, if available, or anchovy paste
1 teaspoon salt
2 teaspoons soy sauce
1 cauliflower, broken into florets, sliced thickly
2 tablespoons hot water

Heat the oil in a wok or frying pan and fry the chiles, onion, garlic and ginger over a low heat, stirring constantly until the onion is soft and golden. Add the shrimp or anchovy paste, fry for 1 minute and then add the salt and the soy sauce. Turn in the cauliflower florets and toss, stirring until they are thoroughly mixed with the onion and chile mixture. Sprinkle with hot water, cover and cook for 10 minutes.

Serve warm or cold but not chilled.
Serves 6

MEXICAN MOLE (pronounced Mollay)

In Mexico this recipe is made with three different kinds of chile (ancho, pasilla and mulato) and is served with white rice, tortillas (soft Mexican pancakes) and beans.

2 chickens, jointed
2 oz lard
3 green chiles, finely sliced
3 small red peppers, finely sliced
8 tomatoes, skinned and chopped
1 tablespoon sesame seeds
2 tablespoons almonds, whole
2 tablespoons dry roast peanuts
1 teaspoon cinnamon
2 cloves garlic, crushed
1¾ pints chicken stock
1 teaspoon sugar
2 oz dark chocolate
cornflour

Joint the chicken and roast it in a moderate oven (180°C, 350°F, Gas Mark 4) for 20 minutes.

Melt the lard in a large saucepan and add the vegetables, seeds, nuts, spices and garlic. Fry gently for 5 minutes. Add the chicken joints, stock, sugar and chocolate. Bring to the boil and simmer for 20 minutes or until the chicken is thoroughly cooked.

Thicken the sauce with a little cornflour, if necessary. Serve with boiled rice.

Serves 8

BRAZILIAN BAKED PORK

The fruit combines with the chile and the pork to give this dish an unusual flavour, which is at the same time sweet but not sweet. It is quite delicious.

good ½ pint chicken stock
1 lb loin or fillet of pork, cubed
1 bay leaf, pinch each of thyme, oregano and ground cloves
4 dried chiles
½ oz walnuts
8 oz green tomatoes
2 oz onions, peeled and chopped
1 clove garlic
2 teaspoons fresh coriander
½ teaspoon salt
½ oz lard
1 pear, peeled, cored and sliced lengthways
1 small banana, peeled and sliced
4 oz cooked peas

In a saucepan, bring the stock to the boil and add the pork, bay, thyme, oregano and cloves. Cover and simmer for 30 minutes or until the pork is almost cooked.

Wash and seed the chiles and tear them in small pieces. Put them in a small bowl and pour over a few spoonfuls of the boiling stock. Leave to soak for 30 minutes.

Pulverise the walnuts in a blender or food processor, add the green tomatoes, onions, garlic, coriander, salt, chiles and the stock in which they were soaked, and blend to a smooth purée.

Melt the lard in a frying pan, add the purée and cook for 5 minutes, stirring constantly. Keep warm.

Drain the juices from the pork and skim off any fat. Pour the stock onto the walnut and tomato purée.

Put the pork in a heavy-based casserole, cover with the fruit and then add the puréed sauce. Cover and cook over a low heat for 30 minutes. Sprinkle over the peas, cook for another 5 minutes to ensure that the peas are warm, and serve at once.
Serves 4

PICKLED CHILES
WITH VEGETABLES

If you are a devotee of piccalilli and other spicy Indian pickles and chutneys, this chile pickle will make a welcome addition to your larder. The pickle will keep for months and can be eaten with cold meats or added to stews.

1 oz green chiles
2 cloves garlic, roughly chopped
½ large carrot, diced
4 oz cauliflower, in florets
1 oz sea salt
1 pint water
14 fl oz wine vinegar
1 stick cinnamon
2 teaspoons cloves
2 teaspoons mace blades
2 teaspoons whole allspice
1 teaspoon pepper corns

If you do not want the pickle too hot, seed the chiles and chop them roughly; if you don't mind the heat, chop them with the seeds.

Put all the vegetables with the salt and the water in a bowl, making sure that the vegetables are immersed (press down with a plate if necessary), and leave for 24 hours.

Put the vinegar and all the spices in a bowl, then cover it with foil, stand it in a saucepan of water and bring to the boil. Remove the pan from the heat and leave to stand for 2 hours.

Remove the vegetables from the brine and rinse, then pack into screw top jars.

Strain the vinegar over the vegetables and seal the jars.

Makes approximately 2 lb pickle

CHILE SHERRY

A recipe from a military gentleman who has been maturing his bottle of chile sherry for 25 years!

1 oz dried chiles
½ pint cooking sherry

Place the chiles in the bottom of a bottle with a tight fitting cork or screw top — an angostura bitters bottle is ideal as it has a 'dropper' on the top. Pour in the sherry, cork the bottle and leave it to mature for from 6 months to 25 years . . .

Use in *very* small quantities as a seasoning in soups and stews.

Top up the bottle with more sherry, as necessary.

THE BOWL OF BLESSEDNESS

CHILE CON CARNE

In the United States the word chile has come to take on an entirely different meaning. From New Mexico to New York, if you ask for chile you get chile con carne — a 'bowl of blessedness' — a rich meaty stew, hotly flavoured with chile peppers.

The origins of this much loved, all-American dish are somewhat confused. The only indisputable fact is that Mexico, the home of the chile pepper, had nothing to do with it! Chile con carne seems to have originated in Texas in the 1850s with the cowboys who were winning the west. They needed solid, warming food, and since beef was abundant and the chiles grew wild in the desert some sort of a stew concocted from the two seemed logical.

The early chile did not contain beans — just beef, water, chiles and spices, boiled together until edible! It is said in Texas that this particular mixture was dished up in the local prisons. So good was the food that ex-cons would commit new crimes simply to get a good bowl of chile!

Whether or not a good chile should contain beans, vegetables other than chiles, spices, nuts or liquor are all matters of dispute in chile-loving circles. The purists maintain that beef (either finely chopped or coarsely minced), chile peppers, cumin, garlic and Mexican oregano are all that is needed for a good chile. Other meats such as pork or chicken are occasionally used for a change. Onions and tomatoes quite often creep in, and less frequently celery and bell peppers.

The question of beans in a chile causes problems. Purists ban them altogether; New Mexicans serve stewed beans as a side dish; Texans add them to the chile. And they all disagree as to what kind of bean should be used — pinto, red, kidney or butter. Even the matter of consistency is disputed — East coast Americans usually like their chile thickened with corn or masa flour, those in the West prefer it thin.

With all this disagreement around it is not surprising that chile-making has now become a national sport. Chile 'cook-offs' are held around America to find the greatest chile cook of the year. Chile appreciation societies abound and 'chiliheads', as they are called, even have their own newspaper . . .

There are as many chile recipes as there are chile lovers. Included here are three very different dishes.

VEGETARIAN CHILE

This recipe would be thrown out by a true chile-lover as it contains neither beef nor beans! However, do not be lulled into a false sense of security — it is plenty hot!

14 oz can tomato juice
8 oz raw bulghur wheat (available in most health food shops)
2 tablespoons olive oil
2 medium-sized onions, coarsely chopped
4 medium-sized cloves garlic, crushed
3 stalks celery and 3 carrots, chopped
2-4 tomatoes, peeled, seeded and chopped
1 tablespoon fresh lemon juice
2 teaspoons salt
2 tablespoons crushed red chiles
1 teaspoon ground cumin
½ teaspoon dried oregano (Mexican if possible)
1½ green bell peppers, cored, seeded and coarsely chopped

Place the tomato juice in a pan and bring to the boil. Remove from the heat and add the wheat. Cover and leave to stand for 15 minutes — the wheat should be slightly crunchy.

Heat the olive oil in a large, heavy saucepan. Add the onions and garlic and cook until soft but not coloured. Add the celery, carrots, tomatoes, lemon juice, salt, chiles, cumin and oregano. Cover and cook until the vegetables are nearly tender. This will take about 15 minutes.

Add the bell peppers and cook for a further 10 minutes. If the chile appears to dry up at any stage, add a little water and stir to prevent sticking.
Serves 8

MIDWEST CHILE

This is a fairly basic chile although it does include onions and tomatoes.

1½ lb stewing beef, coarsely minced
1 large onion, coarsely chopped
2 cloves garlic, finely chopped
1 tablespoon chili powder
1 tablespoon ground cumin
1 teaspoon salt
1 tablespoon tomato purée
4 tablespoons tomato ketchup
1½ lb can tomatoes
5 oz cooked pinto or kidney beans

Put the meat, onion and garlic in a heavy based pan and cook over a medium heat until the meat is evenly browned all over.

Stir in the ground chili, cumin and salt and mix well. Add the tomato purée, ketchup and tomatoes. Bring the mixture to a boil, then lower the heat and simmer, uncovered, for about 1 hour.

Taste and adjust the seasonings. Stir in the beans and simmer, uncovered, for a further 30 minutes.
Serves 6

CHILE EXOTICA

This is one of the more exotic chile recipes and it includes sausages, chocolate and avocado! A true taste experience!

4 oz dried pinto beans
3 tablespoons lard
1 medium-sized onion, coarsely chopped
12 oz spicy pork sausage
1 lb lean beef, coarsely minced
4 cloves garlic, crushed
1 teaspoon anise/aniseeds
½ teaspoon each fennel seeds, ground cloves, ground cinnamon
1 teaspoon black pepper
1 teaspoon paprika pepper
1 teaspoon each ground nutmeg, ground cumin
2 teaspoons dried oregano (Mexican if possible)
4 tablespoons sesame seeds
4 oz ground almonds
3 dried whole chiles, crushed and then soaked in hot water to soften
1½ oz milk chocolate
6 oz can tomato paste
3 tablespoons vinegar
salt
1 avocado pear

Rinse the beans and place in a bowl with 2 pints water. Soak overnight.

Pour the beans and the water into a heavy pan, add

a further pint of water, bring to the boil and simmer, partially covered, for about 45 minutes. The beans should be cooked but firm. Drain, reserving liquid.

Melt 2 tablespoons lard in a heavy pan, add the beans and fry lightly.

Melt the rest of the lard in a heavy pot, add the onion and cook until soft.

In a bowl, combine the sausage and beef with the garlic, anise, fennel, cloves, cinnamon, peppers, nutmeg, cumin and oregano. Add this mixture to the onions, breaking up any lumps with a fork. Fry briskly until the meat is well browned.

Add the reserved bean liquid to the pot and stir in all the remaining ingredients except the beans and the avocado. Bring to the boil and simmer, uncovered, for 30 minutes, stirring occasionally. Add water if the mixture looks too dry — it should be the consistency of a chunky soup.

Add the beans and cook for a further 30 minutes.

Just before serving, adjust seasoning to taste. Slice the avocado over the top of the dish and lightly mix it into the chile.

Serves 8

CULTIVATING CAPSICUMS

If you decide to grow your own bell peppers you should not have too much trouble, provided you have a sheltered sunny corner in the garden or a greenhouse. Chile peppers are less tolerant of northern climates, where they can only be grown in a greenhouse. For both breeds however, the propagation methods are similar.

The seeds (which can be bought at any good garden centre) should be planted during March in pots or trays of sterilised seed compost, and maintained at a temperature of about 16°C/60°F. When the seedlings are large enough to handle, prick them out into 3 inch pots of potting compost. Pot on as necessary. Stand the pots in good light to ensure sturdy, short jointed growth.

If the capsicums are to be grown outside, harden off the plants in a cold frame before planting out in late spring, after the danger of frost has passed. Choose a sheltered sunny spot against a south wall and plant seedlings about 2 feet apart in well-drained, well-manured soil with some superphosphate raked in. But remember that too rich a soil may encourage leaf, not fruit, growth.

Pinch out the growing tips when the plants are

about 6 inches high to encourage a bushy growth. Support the plants and keep the roots moist. Feed once a week with liquid fertiliser.

The flowers will appear in late June or July. Nip out the first ones to encourage fruiting. The fruits should be ready for picking in August and September. Start picking the fruits when they are still green.

If the peppers are to remain in the greenhouse, the seedlings should be potted on into 6 inch and then 8-10 inch pots. They can also be planted in gro-bags. Nip out the flowers as for the outdoor plants, stake them where necessary and syringe the leaves daily during the flowering period to encourage fruit setting.

Water the plants regularly and feed at 10-day intervals once the fruits appear. Keep the atmosphere fairly dry with a minimum night temperature of 18°C/64°F and lightly shade the glass during the hottest months.

Recommended varieties of bell and chile peppers are as follows:-

BELL PEPPERS:
Bell Boy hybrid
California wonder
Canape
Golden calwonder
(yellow when ripe)
Merrimack wonder
New ace
Pimiento (spicy)
Slim pim
World beater
Yolo wonder

CHILE PEPPERS:
Cayenne chili
Hungarian yellow wax
Large cherry
Long red cherry
Long red cayenne

GROWING ORNAMENTAL PEPPERS

The small decorative peppers, like their larger brethren, can be raised from seed, although it is a great deal less risky to buy them pot grown. They will reach a height of 12-13 inches, with woody stems and slightly hairy pointed leaves. They are happiest in bright sunshine and are therefore best positioned in a sunny window. Spray the leaves periodically with clear water, and feed the plant fortnightly during spring until the flowers form. These will be succeeded by glossy red or yellow cone-shaped peppers which will last for about 3 months (perhaps until Christmas) before wrinkling and dropping off.

Like the larger capsicums, different varieties of ornamental pepper produce different coloured fruits. They can be green, white, orange and purple, and may change in colour as they ripen. Ornamental peppers are also available with round bright yellow or purplish-white berry-like fruits. Ornamental capsicum plants do not last more than one year.

With many thanks to
Patricia Harbottle
for all her hard work in
researching the background information
for this book.

If you would like further information on all the titles in this series, and on other Piatkus gift books, please send a stamped addressed envelope to

Judy Piatkus (Publishers) Limited
17 Brook Road,
Loughton, Essex